My First

of
Bible Prayers

Philip Ross

CF4·K

© Copyright 2004 Philip Ross
ISBN: 978-1-85792-944-7

Published in 2004
by
Christian Focus Publications,
Geanies House, Fearn,
Ross-shire, IV20 1TW,
Great Britain.
Reprinted 2005, 2008, 2009, 2011 and 2014

www.christianfocus.com
email:info@christianfocus.com

Cover design by Alister MacInnes
Cover illustrations by Diane Mathes
Publication illustrations by Diane Mathes

Printed and bound by Bell and Bain, Glasgow

MIX
Paper from
responsible sources
FSC
www.fsc.org   FSC® C007785

From the Author

Thousands of years ago, Moses told parents to teach God's words to their children. Eunice was a lady who remembered Moses' instructions. She taught Timothy, her son, so that when he grew up he was able to teach others. His friend, Paul, reminded him that he had known the Bible since he was little. Timothy might not have understood everything when he was young, but the Scriptures made him wise. When he was older, he even went to prison because of his sincere faith in Jesus.

One thing that Timothy learned from the Bible was how to pray. He heard how believers spoke to God and what they asked for. You too need to learn how to pray. Not one of us knows how to pray as we should, but the Bible teaches us and gives us many examples.

Perhaps you already know the Lord's Prayer, which Jesus taught his disciples. In this book, you will find more prayers for you to learn, based on different parts of the Bible. Make them your own. God promises to answer.

Most of the prayers are short and will not be too hard to remember. Some are a little longer and will need a bit more effort. Below every prayer are a few sentences, to help you understand what it is about. If you want to learn more, you can look up the part of the Bible where the words come from. Sometimes, you will need someone to explain things to you.

You will learn different names and titles for God. You will worship him as your Creator, Saviour, and King. You will admit your badness and sin. You will ask for everything that you need to make you good and bring you to heaven.

Remember that Jesus said, "If you ask for anything in my name, I will do it."

Philip Ross

My First Book of Bible Prayers is a wonderful guide for children – and for their parents! Indeed it helps 'children of all ages' to take the first steps towards the Heavenly Father, with words we can use to speak to him.

Philip Ross is well qualified to give us the help we need. Brought up in a lively Christian home where prayer was made because God was loved, he and his wife are now creating a similar environment for their own youngsters. They know from experience that the Heavenly Father's word is to be trusted and that he hears and answers prayer.

Give your children this outstanding little book, and use it with them. It might well be one of the most important things you could ever do as a parent.

Sinclair B. Ferguson
Associate Minister, St Peter's Free Church,
Dundee

Learning to pray the text of Scripture and to apply its truth to our lives is vital for our spiritual growth.

This book by Philip Ross enables children to do both. I can't recommend this wonderful tool more highly.

C.J. Mahaney
Senior Pastor
Sovereign Grace Church
Louisville, USA

We have best understood the Bible when we turn it into prayer. That is what Philip Ross does for children in "My First Book of Bible Prayers." He takes brief texts of Scripture and turns them into simple, and yet profound prayers that children can readily use. This little booklet will open the heavens for many at a young age. As a father of a large family, I wish this rich spiritual resource had been available to me twenty years ago!

Dr. Douglas F. Kelly
Richard Jordan Professor of Theology
RTS Charlotte
North Carolina, USA

1

Lord Jesus, the First and the Last,
in the beginning
you laid the foundations
of the earth,
and the heavens
are the work of your hands.
They will perish,
but you will remain.

Acts 7:59; Revelation 1:17; Psalm 102:25;
Hebrews 1:10-11

Some day God will destroy the whole world.
Nothing will be left. Even Mount Everest
will melt away like wax on a candle. But
the Lord Jesus will never go
away. He was here before
Mount Everest. He made
everything. And when
everything has gone, he
will still be here. You can
only be safe with him.

2

Everlasting God,
my life is like a mist
that appears for a little while
and then it is gone;
teach me to count my days
so that I will gain a wise heart.

James 4:14; Psalm 90:2, 12

Go outside on a frosty morning and you will see your breath. But pay attention! As soon as it leaves your mouth, it will disappear. You cannot get it back. Your life is like that. Is it hard to understand that your life is so short? Then ask God to teach you and make you wise.

3

God of Jacob, my refuge,
be with me and keep me
in the way that I go.
Give me bread to eat
and clothes to wear.

Psalm 46:7; Genesis 28:20

One night God spoke to Jacob. "I am
with you", he said. "I will watch over
you wherever you go." Jacob believed
God. God took care of
him. Do you ask God to
look after you? If you
believe his
promises,
he will
always
provide
for you.

4

Behold, I was born in iniquity,
and in sin
my mother conceived me.

Psalm 51:5

Do you ever wonder, "Why do I keep doing
bad things?" Perhaps you think, "The
problem is, I am bad." Yes, you are.
But, you need to tell God all
about it. Admit that you
were never good. Not
even when you were tiny.
He knows when we only
pretend to be good.

5

O God, you will not despise
a broken and a contrite heart.
Be merciful to me a sinner.

Psalm 51:17; Luke 18:13

You know that God hates you doing wrong.
But do you hate it? Do you feel sad to have
offended God? Then you should tell him.
God will always love
you if you cry in your
heart about your
sin. And when you
ask him to forgive
you, he will be very
kind.

6

Give me an honest
and good heart,
so that when I hear your word,
I will remember it
and bear fruit.

Luke 8:15

God's word
is like seed.
It can only
grow in good
ground. The
trouble is that
our hearts are like
bad ground. But
if God gives you a
good heart, you will hear and remember
his word. You will keep it in mind and
always produce good fruit.

7

Faithful God,
call me into the fellowship
of your Son,
Jesus Christ our Lord.

1 Corinthians 1:9

Perhaps someone once asked you, "Will
you be my friend?" but you did not listen.
Or, you said, "Yes, I will be your friend,"
but you soon forgot one another. It is
different with God.
Even if you are far
away, you will hear
when he calls you
to be close to
his Son. He will
always keep you
in his family.

8

Whom have I in heaven but you?
And there is nothing on earth
that I desire besides you.

Psalm 73:25

Have you noticed that very bad people
often have good things and
not much trouble? If
God is your guide, you
know that these people
will not live happily
forever. You see that
only God can give you
joy that lasts. Do you
want him more than
anything else?

9

I love you LORD,
because you have heard my voice
and my cries for mercy.

Psalm 116:1

Lots of people cry to the LORD when they
are in trouble. But when their problems
go away they forget about
him. Do not be like that.
Call on the LORD for
as long as you
live. And when
he helps you,
say,
"I love you
LORD."

10

O LORD of hosts,
our sun and shield;
give me grace and glory
to go on from strength to strength
until I appear before you
in your dwelling-place.

Psalm 84

Sometimes following God is like being
away from home. You want to go back,
but it is too far and too
difficult. You need God
to guide and protect
you. He rules from
heaven. And when
the journey gets
harder, he will
make you stronger.
Then, one day you
will be at home with him.

11

Lord of Glory,
let your glorious name
be blessed forever.
Let the whole earth
be filled with your glory.

1 Corinthians 2:8; Psalm 72:19

Jesus is not like other kings. Most people
do not see how great he is. Has God shown
you Jesus?   Then you
will never see anyone
greater. You want
everyone to realize
that no one is more
wonderful. You want
the whole world to
see Jesus' glory.

12

LORD, you are the Rock,
your work is perfect,
all your ways are justice.
You are a God of faithfulness
and without iniquity,
you are just and upright.

Deuteronomy 32:4

Do you trust everyone? Probably not.
Some people are mean and
twisted. There is one
person who can always
be trusted: the LORD.
He is always honest,
fair, and reliable. He
is absolutely perfect.
If you want to be safe,
stay close to him.

13

LORD, you are our judge,
our lawgiver,
and our king.
Save us.

Isaiah 33:22

Christian people cannot do anything
without Jesus. No one else is wise enough
to guide us. Whenever we make our own
rules, we end up in a big mess.
The men who lead us
die or fail. But the
LORD reigns forever.
He is the only one
who can save his people.

14

O Lord our God,
to us belongs open shame
because we have
sinned against you,
but to you belong
mercy and forgiveness.

Daniel 9:8-9

Daniel was a good man. He loved God's
people. They were suffering because they
turned away from God. Can you imagine
how sad that made Daniel? He felt
ashamed. But he spoke to God
about all their failures.
Daniel understood
that although
God corrects
his children,
he never leaves
them.

15

O LORD, the God of truth,
if I say that I have no sin,
I deceive myself,
and the truth is not in me.

Psalm 31:5; 1 John 1:8

If you have black hair, but you say, "I am sure my hair is red," you will not trick anyone. Everyone sees your black hair. In the same way, you cannot make God think that you do nothing wrong. He sees everything. Admit the truth about yourself.

16

God and Father
of our Lord Jesus Christ,
draw me to your Son
or else I will be
unable to come to him.

1 Peter 1:3; John 6:44

Suppose you offered something good to someone, but they would not take it. Jesus said that we are all like that with him. He offers himself, but you cannot come to Jesus unless God the Father gives you the power. That is why you need to ask for his help.

17

Good Shepherd, feed me,
gather me like a lamb in your arms,
and carry me in your bosom.

John 10:11; Isaiah 40:11

Long ago God chose kings and leaders to
be like good shepherds. But often they
took care of themselves and not God's
people. Then God promised
that he would come to
look after them himself.
And he did. Our Lord
Jesus is the perfect
shepherd. You can trust
him to look after you. He
even gave his life for the
sheep.

18

God of hope,
fill me with joy
and peace
in believing.

Romans 15:13

Are you only
happy when
good things are
happening? Not
if you trust in God.
Then you can be
glad even when life
is hard. You believe
his wonderful promises
for the future, so you do
not need to worry. And no matter what
happens, God fills you with joy.

19

Give me neither poverty
nor riches;
feed me with the food
that I need.

Proverbs 30:8

People think that money makes you happy.
Hardly anyone wants to be poor. But it is
good to be neither rich nor poor. Being
rich is dangerous. You might
forget that you need
God. That does not
mean it is good to
be poor. Then you
might steal. It is
best to have just
what you need.

20

God of all comfort,
Father of mercies,
strengthen me to the end,
so that I will be blameless
on the day
of our Lord Jesus Christ.

2 Corinthians 1:3; 1 Corinthians 1:8

One day the Lord Jesus will return to judge everyone. Will you be perfect when he comes? Only if you understand that you are weak. Then you will ask God for strength to do what is right. He is a sympathetic Father who always encourages his children.

21

I bow before you, the LORD, the LORD, a God merciful and gracious, slow to anger, and abounding in loving-kindness and truth. You keep loving-kindness for thousands, forgiving iniquity and transgression and sin. But you will by no means clear the guilty, visiting the iniquity of the fathers on the children and the children's children, to the third and fourth generation.

Exodus 34:6-8

What kind of person is God? He is greater than you can imagine. When his children go astray, he still loves them. He forgives all kinds of evil. Think of how kind he is. But remember that he never ignores our guilt. What you do matters. It affects you and others.

22

My iniquities are more than
the hairs of my head;
my heart fails me.
Be pleased, O LORD,
to deliver me!
O LORD,
come quickly to help me!

Psalm 40:12-13

It is difficult to count the hairs on
your head. It is even harder to count
your sins. They are more than the hairs
on your head. And they
cause you such trouble.
Have you discovered
that? Then you know
that the LORD needs
to take away your sin.
Who else can rescue
you?

23

Like a newborn baby,
may I long for
the pure milk of the word.
Then I will taste
and see that you are good.

1 Peter 2:1-3; Psalm 34:8

Tiny babies love to drink milk. Are you like that with the Bible? God's Word will make you grow and keep you right. As you believe his promises, you will discover that he is good. The LORD will rescue you from trouble. He will make sure that you have whatever is good for you.

24

Give me your Spirit
so that I will cry,
"You are my Father, my God,
and the Rock of my salvation."

Romans 8:15; Psalm 89:26-27

God keeps his children safe. He is like a rock. Nothing blows him around. But he is not hard and cold. Jesus  called him "Father". Do you? If you ask him, God will give you his Spirit. King Jesus, his firstborn, will be your brother. And you too will call God "Father".

25

Teach me to do everything
without grumbling or arguing
so that I may be blameless
and innocent – shining
like a light in the world.

Philippians 2:14-15

It is easy to complain and argue. Everyone
does. But you should be different. You
must be pure like Jesus.
He was not selfish. When
he was badly treated,
he did not grumble.
If you are like him,
you will shine like a
bright star in the
night sky.

26

God of heaven,
help me to submit to you
and resist the devil
so that he will flee from me.

Nehemiah 1:4; James 4:7

The devil is powerful. He works hard
to make you disobey God. But he is also
a coward. He knows that you will fight
against him when he sees that
you serve God. And when you
do that, Satan will run
away. The devil
always loses
when the God
of heaven is on
your side.

27

O Lord my God,
please help me to love you
with all my heart,
and with all my soul,
and with all my mind.
And help me to love my neighbour
as myself.

Deuteronomy 6: 5; Leviticus 19: 18;
Mark 12:29-31

God gave his people
laws so that they
would know how to
behave. You can
read them in the
first books of the
Bible. They will teach

you that God expects you to love him as
completely as he loves his own children.
He also wants you to care about others as
much as you care about yourself.

28

God of our Lord Jesus Christ,
Father of glory,
I want to know Christ
and the power
of his resurrection.

Ephesians 1:17; Philippians 3:10

God raised Jesus from the dead. He is alive. Knowing Jesus is not the same as remembering a dead person. It is like being with someone who is full of life. If you trust in Jesus then nothing is more important to you than knowing him. You want his power to change your life.

29

God of the living,
use me to lead many
to righteousness
so that I will shine
like the sun in your kingdom.

Matthew 13:41-43; 22:32; Daniel 12:2-3

Will it be a good day for you, when God raises the dead? It depends what kind of person you are now. If you do not love God, it will be dreadful. But if you are someone who teaches others to follow him, it will be a wonderful day. God will change you. He will make you splendid forever.

30

LORD, you never slumber or sleep.
Watch over me
when I go out
and when I come in.
Protect me day and night,
now and for evermore.

Psalm 121

Soldiers die, or ships sink, if someone
who should be looking out for danger falls
asleep. You cannot trust anyone to stay
awake, except the LORD. He never gets
sleepy and he sees every
danger you will meet.
Whatever may
happen, he
can protect
you. Trust no
one else with
your life.

31

You are my God,
and I will give thanks to you;
you are my God;
I will exalt you.
Give thanks to the LORD
for his loving kindness
lasts forever.

Psalm 118:28-29

The Bible tells how God divided the Red
Sea for the Israelites. They walked across
on dry land to escape Pharaoh.
Even more amazing is that
the Father sent his Son
to be the Saviour of
the world. It is better
to trust in him than
anyone else. He saves
us from death. Do you
thank him for that?

32

Worthy are you, our Lord and God,
to receive glory
and honour
and power,
for you created all things,
and by your will,
they existed and were created.

Revelation 4:11

At times, the world seems to be out of
control. But if you could look into heaven,
what would you see? Something too
wonderful to describe: God sitting on a
throne. Nothing exists unless he made it.
Nothing happens unless he allows it. That
 is why all of heaven never
stops worshipping him,
and you must do the
same.

33

LORD, you are our Father,
we are the clay,
and you are our potter;
we are all the work of your hand.
Be not so terribly angry, O LORD,
and remember not
iniquity forever.

Isaiah 64:8-9

Churches become weak when the LORD's
people wander from his ways. Does
that make you sad? Then you
should cry to God for
help. Remind him that
he made the church
and it is his family.
Ask him to forgive us
because Jesus came
down from heaven to
save his people.

34

My heart is deceitful above all things
and desperately sick.
Heal me, O LORD,
and I shall be healed;
save me
and I shall be saved,
for you are the one I praise.

Jeremiah 17:9, 14

The LORD is a fountain of living water. He satisfies us and gives us endless life. So why do we turn away from him? It is because our hearts are

sick. We fool ourselves into thinking that we can succeed without God. Thankfully, he knows our crazy thoughts and is able to make us completely better.

35

Do not remember the sins of my youth
or my transgressions;
remember me according to
your loving kindness,
for the sake of your goodness,
O LORD.

Psalm 25:7

God is not forgetful. He is able to remember everything. That is bad news because we have sinned against God. It is also good news since he never forgets to be merciful. We know that because, by his blood, Jesus freed his people from their sins. That means you can ask him to forget your sins.

36

Give me faith to believe
that the Son of God
loved me
and gave himself
for me.

Galatians 2:20

What will make God accept you? Not the
good things you do. Jesus alone can make
you good enough for God. You must believe
that he loved you and gave his
life for you. There is no
other way to please
God.

37

O LORD,
the God of Israel,
our Father,
forever and ever,
you are spirit;
help me to worship you
in spirit and in truth.

1 Chronicles 29:10; John 4:24

You cannot see God. He is spirit. So how can you worship him? Only with the help of his Spirit and as the Bible teaches you. That means you can only worship God through Jesus. You need his Holy Spirit to show you that Jesus is the truth.

38

Send your Holy Spirit
to teach me all things
and remind me of
everything Jesus said.

John 14:26

After Jesus was on earth, he asked his
Father to send the Holy Spirit to his
disciples. The Spirit came. He helped
them to talk and write about what Jesus
said and did. You still need to ask for the
Spirit's help. Without
him, you will never
really understand
what they wrote in
the Bible.

39

My God, my God,
why have you forsaken me?
Why are you so far from saving me,
from the words of my groaning?
O my God, I cry by day,
but you do not answer,
and by night, but I find no rest.

Psalm 22:1-2; Matthew 27:46

Do you ever keep praying and nothing
happens? Perhaps you think God has
forgotten you. Feeling like that can bring
you to know Jesus better. When
he was being crucified, he
felt that God had left him.
That is why you can
be certain God
always rescues
those who
trust in him.

40

LORD, help me to trust in you
with all my heart
and not to lean upon
my own understanding.

Proverbs 3:5

What do you think of yourself? Are you
wise? If you think you are wise, then
you are not. It is a mistake to imagine
that you are clever enough to make your

own plans. You will
only be wise when
you completely
trust in the LORD
and not at all in
yourself.

41

Shepherd and Guardian of my soul,
I have gone astray
like a lost sheep.
Seek your servant,
for I do not forget
your commandments.

1 Peter 2:25; Psalm 119:176

Travelling somewhere for the first time,
you might not notice if you get lost. But
by the hundredth journey, you know when
you make a mistake. The
better you know God's
commands, the sooner
you will realise when
you go wrong. The good
news is that Jesus
came to save the lost.
He protects the lives
of his people.

42

God our Saviour,
I brought nothing into the world
and I can take nothing out of it.
If I have food and clothing,
make me content with that.

1 Timothy 1:1; 6:7-8

Those who want to get rich do not love
Jesus. And when they get into the church,
they quarrel and only help themselves.
But if God is your Saviour, you understand

that anything you gain
from the world will be
left behind when you
die. So you should be
happy with whatever
he gives you and
wherever he puts
you.

43

LORD,
help me to do what you require:
to act justly,
to love mercy,
and to walk humbly with you,
my God.

Micah 6:8

What does the LORD expect of you? You might think that going to church is what matters. But God hates it when you sing and pray if you do not want to do what is right every day. If you say you love him, he expects you to love others and to remember that he is your King.

44

God of gods and Lord of lords,
the great, the mighty,
and the awesome God,
from the rising sun
to where it sets,
let your name be great
among the nations.

Deuteronomy 10:17; Malachi 1:11

All over the world, Jesus is worshipped
as God. He is greater than all other gods.
There is no one like him. He is powerful,
merciful, and fair. You can pray that
everyone would learn that
he is Lord of lords. God
promised that people
in every place would
worship him.

45

I will give thanks to you, O Lord,
among the peoples;
I will sing praises to you
among the nations.
For your loving-kindness
reaches the heavens,
your faithfulness to the clouds.

Psalm 57:9-10

The Lord will never love you in a small way.
You cannot measure his constant kindness.
It would be easier to take a ruler and work
out the distance to the sun. The
proper thing to do is to
thank him. The whole
world must
know that no
other god
is like our
God.

46

Give me this confidence in you,
that if I ask for anything
according to your will,
you will hear me.

1 John 5:14

God is a father who gives his children
anything they ask for. It is not that you
can make God do whatever you like. It is
because if you are one of his
children, you want what
he wants. So when you
pray, you love to ask for
things that please him.
You can be sure that
he hears.

47

Keep me on the path
of the righteous,
which like the light of dawn,
shines brighter and brighter
until the full day.

Proverbs 4:18

If you live to please God, then you listen
to his words and keep his commands. They
show you the way to go. Forget to follow
his directions and you will get
lost in the dark. But if
you remember his
teaching, you will
grow wiser and
stronger until you
see God.

48

Work in me
so that I will be able
to choose what is best
and so be pure and blameless
in the day of Jesus Christ.

Philippians 1:10

Is God doing his good work in you? Then you love to please him. Not to break his law is good, but that is the least you want to do. You long to give him everything because Jesus is coming soon. When he comes, will he see that you chose the best things for the best reasons?

49

King of kings and
Lord of lords,
clothe yourself
with splendour and majesty.
Ride forth victoriously;
let your right hand display
awesome deeds.

Revelation 19:16; Psalm 45:3-4

Jesus is a warrior. But he is no ordinary
soldier. He fights for truth and
righteousness. Jesus never loses. His
enemies looked strong when he was
crucified, but Satan could not hold our
Saviour. No one who fights
against Jesus can succeed.
One day everyone will
realise that he is the
great and powerful King.

50

Let me hear your voice today.
Do not let me harden my heart
because I want to
enter your rest.

Psalm 95:8, 11; Hebrews 3-4

In the past, God spoke to his people through men like Moses. But sometimes his people would not believe, so they could not receive the things he promised. It is even more important for us to pay attention because God has spoken to us by sending his Son. If you want to enjoy heaven, you must believe him.

Memory record

Tick each book once you have learned each prayer.

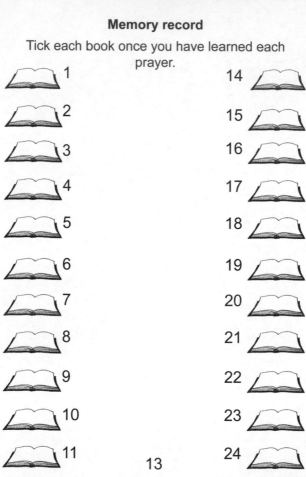

1	14
2	15
3	16
4	17
5	18
6	19
7	20
8	21
9	22
10	23
11	24
12	13 25

Memory record

Tick each book once you have learned each prayer.

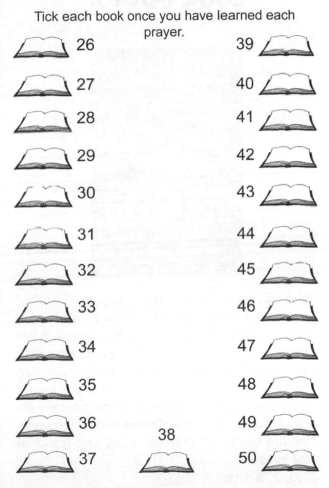

26
27
28
29
30
31
32
33
34
35
36
37
38
39
40
41
42
43
44
45
46
47
48
49
50

Look out for

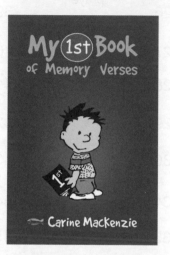

Children have amazing minds. Access their God given intelligence and help them to memorise His word. The truth that we learn as children will stick in our minds and can be brought back to our memory at vital stages in later life. Scripture memorising is not just an insurance policy for the future, but a wonderful provision for the daily life of young and old. This will prove to be a priceless treasure to our children for today and for all of their lives.

ISBN: 978-1-85792-783-2

Look out for

If you have ever wanted to know how to explain the Christian faith to young children in bite-sized chunks, then 'My 1st Book of Questions & Answers' will be of great help to you. In 114 profound questions and answers, backed by scripture proofs, best selling author Carine Mackenzie provides an invaluable tool to get you started.

ISBN: 978-1-85792-570-8

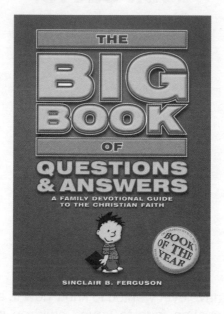

This book by Sinclair Ferguson is a book for families to discover the key doctrines of Christianity in a way that stimulates discussion and helps children want to know more.

Winner of Christian Children's Book of the Year

ISBN: 978-1-85792-295-0

Colour The Bible

These colouring books help children to learn the books of the Bible and improve their hand eye coordination at the same time. An excellent tool and resource for Sunday schools and churches.

ISBN: 978-1-85792-761-0

ISBN: 978-1-85792-762-7

ISBN: 978-1-85792-763-4

ISBN: 978-1-85792-764-1

ISBN: 978-1-85792-765-8

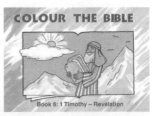

ISBN: 978-1-85792-766-5

CHRISTIAN FOCUS PUBLICATIONS

Christian Focus Publications publishes books for adults and children under its four main imprints: Christian Focus, CF4K, Mentor and Christian Heritage. Our books reflect our conviction that God's Word is reliable and Jesus is the way to know him, and live for ever with him.

Our children's publication list includes a Sunday School curriculum that covers pre-school to early teens, and puzzle and activity books. We also publish personal and family devotional titles, biographies and inspirational stories that children will love.

If you are looking for quality Bible teaching for children then we have an excellent range of Bible stories and age-specific theological books.

From pre-school board books to teenage apologetics, we have it covered!

**Find us at our web page:
www.christianfocus.com**